LEADING WITH NON-VIOLENCE IN A WORLD SURROUNDED BY IDIOTS

The Code Of Effective Public Speaking And Little Tricks For Crucial Conversations To Boost Sales

By

I0422242

ROCKY RICHARDSON

Copyright©2024.ROCKY.RICHARDSON

TABLE OF CONTENT

FOREWORDS

It has been a matter of contention for many because individuals often fail to completely appreciate the benefits of effective communication. In order to create and expand a profitable company, it is important to have a solid understanding of effective communication within the appropriate environment. There are certain methods that may assist you in improving your communication abilities, and these methods will identify the areas in which you are deficient in both speaking and listening effectively.

Gaining the ability to communicate effectively is crucial if you want to advance in your work. Your whole plan to advance will fail if you are unable to communicate properly, regardless of what you do or what your objectives are. Without an efficient communication strategy, it is impossible to convey your ideas and objectives.

Effective communication involves using strong communication strategies to essentially brainwash people into acting in a certain manner. In order to stay in that position, a leader must possess strong communication abilities. A person who has a significant position in an organization or a department within it is considered a leader. Leaders of organizations and teams, as well as those in the political, religious, and local spheres, are also present.

People will assume that if you are puzzled while describing something, they will be confused when they try to do it as well. This is a gesture that comes naturally to everyone who is normal. As you've probably seen, there are certain individuals who speak with such assurance and alertness that they consistently seem to be more successful and in control of their life than those who lack these qualities.

This isn't because individuals of the second kind are incapable of working; rather, it's simply that they are unable to successfully persuade others to collaborate with them or operate as a team. There are certain ways that may aid in improving your ability to communicate effectively. These approaches will identify your areas of weakness in both speaking and listening.

Some people believe that communication just consists of speaking and expressing themselves, but you should be aware that listening is also a crucial component of communication. You may then express yourself as you listen, and the speaker may be encouraged or discouraged to continue speaking as a result of your emotions. I will attempt to cover every significant strategy in this E-book to assist you become a more successful communicator and increase its effectiveness for you.

This tutorial will focus on business leaders and how effective communication is a critical component of strong leadership. We'll also discuss what makes a strong leader, including how to be identified by their decisions and communication style. Learn all you need right here.

CHAPTER 1:

COMMUNICATION BASIC

Gaining proficiency in communication is an absolutely essential ability if you want to advance in your work. Your whole plan to advance will fail if you are unable to communicate properly, regardless of what you do or your goals.

Any company venture, no matter how large or little, must prioritize building and maintaining a solid personnel base. Thus, maintaining effective communication is essential to keeping everyone content and operating. A clear image of what is anticipated and wanted is created when there is effective communication between all parties, allowing information to be disclosed and accepted without difficulty.

When there is no communication, there is a genuine chance that issues may arise since people are acting alone and not collaborating as a team. This frequently has unpleasant and most probably negative effects. A person with strong communication skills will also be easier to establish in the commercial world, laying the groundwork for authority and respect in that specific endeavor.

Because of the excellent communication provided, this will also aid to guarantee that clients will be more than happy to produce repeat business. Transmitting information is only one aspect of communication; another is listening intently. When the communication tone demonstrates that the company owner is aware of the demands of the clients, it is highly valued by them and will undoubtedly be warmly accepted.

The fact that effective communication guarantees fewer errors is another crucial thing to keep in mind. Ignoring its significance may ultimately result in expensive errors, from which recovery may be difficult. Without communication, we would not be able to share our experiences with other people. Communication is a vital activity that enables us to express our emotions.

CHAPTER 2:

TYPES OF COMMUNICATION

Two forms of communication exist, which may be classified as verbal and non-verbal communication. These two are essential since they complement each other. Verbal communication has several characteristics, including words, language, voice, and others. A child has voice chords from birth, and as he develops, he learns to control them and produce words.

Some words are simple natural expressions, like laughing or crying out. He eventually picks up the language, however. them by themselves have no meaning; instead, people give them meaning by arranging them in various combinations.

We usually try to make things plain when we communicate, but this doesn't always happen. When we think something is important to us, we also tend to expect that others should find it similarly important, but this is not always the case. Speaking may present many challenges, and the only way to overcome them is to gain experience.

Speaking may be divided into two main categories: public speaking and interpersonal speaking. Interpersonal speaking is most prevalent as most of our communication is one-on-one, and accurate reading and understanding of others are prerequisites for doing so. In interpersonal communication, manners are crucial, and you should communicate in a way that won't insult the other person in any way.

You can't become better at public speaking by merely watching other people who do it well. History has shown that although some people are really gifted public speakers, others are not.

Additionally essential to communication is nonverbal communication, which in some situations may even be more important than verbal communication. There may be circumstances in which using words to adequately communicate something is impossible. In these cases, nonverbal communication is useful. Nonverbal communication consists of several components, such as haptic cues, artifacts, chronemics, and other related elements. The most important items are called artifacts, and they include jewelry, clothes, accessories, and other items that shape your identity.

The majority of specialists believe that your clothing is the most important haptic element and that it consistently conveys your true personality. People may often be assessed based just on the clothes they wear. Likewise, haptic feedback may also give you a sense of emotions. You should use extreme caution since how you touch someone or anything might convey the incorrect message.

CHAPTER 3:

EFFECTIVE VERBAL COMMUNICATION

We sometimes take verbal communication for granted because everyone can communicate, even if they are not proficient writers. However, not everyone is inherently good at verbal communication. Thankfully, with a little time and effort, it is a talent that can be taught.

The Significance of Spoken Expression

There is more to spoken language than merely unambiguous information conveyance. What is said and how the audience interprets it may also be influenced by the delivery's style and tone. Any leader should work on developing the ability to communicate succinctly and effectively both in person and on the phone. A competent leader must also be aware of the distinctions between the two as well as other factors that affect communication outside of words and phrases.

In-person Communication

One of the most effective methods to spread ideas and encourage conversation is via face-to-face communication. That may not be the most effective method for providing comprehensive information, however. When it comes to organizing new projects and initiatives, understanding the distinction between the two may often make the difference between success and failure. For instance, although having face-to-face conversations is wonderful, it is not an effective approach to ensure that tasks are completed accurately to hurry into a discussion as you pass someone's desk. It would be best to send an email or have a formal meeting.

Body Language

Your communication style and personal identity might be inferred from your body language. Ignorance of body language may sometimes work against you and the message you were attempting to deliver. When your spoken words and body language diverge significantly, it may be confusing to others and give the impression that you are not speaking the truth or are upset.

For instance, crossing your arms in front of your chest while speaking or listening might send many unfavorable signals. If you don't stare at them or turn sideways, your audience may assume you are defensive, angry, or uninterested.

Additionally, folded arms convey the message that others should avoid you. People may never ask for what they need since your body language already looks to be telling them no, and they may even suggest stubbornness or resistance.

Be Organic

When you are interacting with someone face-to-face, a more easygoing and natural body position with your arms resting freely at your sides is much more welcome.

Avoid playing around while you talk. Practice being silent. Keep your eyes open. Look around the room if you are among a big gathering of people. Avoid pacing, but do make necessary movements. Nod in agreement as you listen. Pay close attention. Avoid trying to talk first. Hold off till the individual is done. Then, to make sure you have heard the question properly and in case somebody hasn't, repeat what you believe to be its main points.

Voice Tone

Whether speaking, tone of voice matters a lot, especially whether speaking over the phone or in person. Saying "Thanks for joining us" at the start of the meeting, for instance, may come off as genuine and kind. Saying "Thanks" with emphasis to someone who is arriving 20 minutes late, on the other hand, might come out as very sardonic and perhaps even impolite.

Comparably, saying "Thanks a lot" aloud and reading it on a paper have distinct connotations. It might be a caustic remark or a statement of thanks. Voice tone is crucial.

Organizing and Conducting Presentations and Meetings

It is inevitable for a company leader to oversee meetings and deliver presentations at some point. Your reputation as an effective leader may depend on how successfully you perform in this role. Your leadership won't be questioned if you are a well-organized leader with a defined agenda who can move a meeting forward quickly and effectively while producing desired results.

However, these sessions will not be fruitful and will damage your image as a strong leader if they degenerate into meaningless back-and-forth debates and no work gets done.

Presenting information with PowerPoint decks, these days many firms rely entirely on their decks for success. It is crucial that you concentrate on this ability in order to prepare and deliver presentations that will keep audiences engaged, convince, and educate them rather than putting them to sleep.

Speaking in Public

During meetings, conferences, presentations, and other events, you will need to speak in front of both big and small audiences. According to studies, most people's greatest dread is public speaking; the fear of dying comes in third. This implies that most individuals would prefer to be in the casket than to deliver the eulogy over it, as someone once quipped.

But it docsn't have to be that way. To improve your public speaking skills and deliver speeches with more assurance and impact, there are several methods to practice. All you need to do is commit the necessary time and energy to practicing until you achieve perfection. If you believe that this is a personal weakness that needs to be addressed in order to become a better communicator and leader, then even if you are not perfect, you can still perform much better than you are now.

Communicating Self-Belief

Being a confident presenter is crucial because, if you project confidence in both your appearance and your voice, your audience will sense that you are speaking the truth and not hiding anything.

Returning to the earlier example of needing to announce impending layoffs, if you convey a positive message about this being a necessary development for the company's strength moving ahead, people will feel much more secure about the company's future. Your audience will get uneasy if you come off as hesitant, anxious, or doubtful about the need of taking these actions.

Motivating Your Viewers

People are inspired to follow great leaders. If Julius Caesar had felt insecure or had shrugged his shoulders and said, "Well, maybe it will work out," he would never have crossed the Rubicon and became the ruler of the Roman Empire. In its place, he said, "I came, I saw, I conquered."

Every organization will have some leaders who set the standard and serve as sources of inspiration for others. You may still set the tone and take the lead on projects and initiatives even if your present position does not currently require you to exercise leadership duties.

When it's time for your end-of-year review or you decide to ask for a raise, it will be simple to show off your leadership potential if you are ready to do so and can motivate others to follow you. You may use your accomplishments as tangible proof of your accomplishments.Face-to-face communication is essential for achieving goals and developing a shared understanding of the company's ideals because of all these factors. Calls might also be beneficial.

Efficient Telephone Conversations

Talking over the phone may be a quick method to accomplish tasks, but if you're not clear about what you want to talk about at the beginning and what you want to get out of the call, it can also lead to misunderstanding.

While chatting is excellent, you might find that you are talking in circles at times. It's also possible that after seeming to agree on a certain course of action, you discover that the person you were chatting with had forgotten that aspect of the discussion. This implies that even though you could anticipate something significant to be completed, it never does.

Organizing phone interactions as far in advance as possible is the best strategy. In the event that you must make any "cold calls"—that is, attempt to conduct business with strangers—ascertain their degree of interest and request a follow-up call at a time that is convenient for them, as well as an email address where you can reach them.

Avoid attempting to advance like a charging bull. As a consequence, you can just get a no and lose the chance to engage in a fruitful discussion. Everyone is busy, but journalists in particular. For example, if you phone them to pitch a story and attempt to get right into your pitch while they are on deadline, you will probably receive a "no, and don't call again."

However, if you give them a call and inquire about a suitable time to chat and if they have a deadline, they will realize that you are aware of their time limits and working environment. Asking when would be a good time to call back and if they would like to be contacted by phone or email might help you proceed if you explain that you would want to pitch a story.

If you decide to arrange a follow-up call, plan beforehand. Make a list of talking points before every call. One by one, cross them all out. As required, take notes. Consider using dictation software, like dictation.io, if you are concerned that you may miss anything. You will only be able to record your side of the discussion, it is true, but at least you will have your perspective. If necessary, you may make notes on what they say.

Review your notes after the talk and write them up so they make sense. Once you are certain that your recap of the conversation is correct, thank the other person by email for their time. Please email a copy of your notes.

Emphasize any necessary follow-ups, deadlines, or action items in particular. You may make sure that you both understand what was stated in this manner. Inquire if they had any other questions or if there was anything you missed. Request that they include it in the email or set up a different call.

After they have provided feedback, you will have a shared document and "paper trail" with all of the key issues covered during the phone conversation. After then, you may use it to monitor development, draft a new contract, revise an old one, and so on. This is a good way to introduce the idea of written communication's significance in your leadership tactics. In the next chapters, let's examine this.

CHAPTER 4:

EFFECTIVE NON-VERBAL COMMUNICATION

We covered the value of in-person and phone discussions in the last chapter as a way to convey ideas. Nonetheless, written agreements are necessary in formal commercial transactions. Make sure that anything you write is understandable and/or agreed upon by making sure it is succinct, clear, and grammatically accurate. Throughout your career as a company leader, you will need to produce a variety of written works. Among them will be:

- Email correspondence
- Letters
- PowerPoint demonstrations
- lists of things to accomplish
- Lists of Checks
- Plans for businesses
- Commercial propositions
- Project details
- Job descriptions
- Shareholder Reports
- Outlines for fresh projects
- Talks
- news releases

Many individuals detest writing, yet the fact is that leaders who are adept at communicating clearly in writing and targeting the appropriate audience will be more successful.

Make Use of Your Content

Writing the fundamentals once and repurposing them as required is one of the finest strategies to quickly produce quality written content. Store all of your most crucial correspondence in files and folders with clear labels. You should have easy access to documents such as your mission statement, quarterly reports, and company strategy. You can effortlessly adapt your greatest PowerPoint presentations to a variety of scenarios.

Maintain Excellent Records

Effective leaders have excellent organizational skills. For each significant project, keep a paper trail with names, dates, times, locations, emails, receipts, and more. If you are managing a company, they are crucial for tax considerations. They also act as a backup in case your computers malfunction and you require printed copies of each of these things.

Keep track of all of your paper and digital filing.

All of your most significant contracts should be kept in at least two paper copies: one for storage and one for reference and possible copying. Organize your emails and PC. Store your documents correctly filed in a fireproof cabinet so you can quickly access critical documents when needed.

To make sure nothing is ever lost, make use of cloud-based storage and backup hard drives. Additionally, consider what would occur if you were ever the victim of anything. Naturally, we are not essential. However, if you are well organized, it will make things much simpler for anybody else in the firm who needs to take over your responsibilities in the case of an accident or illness God forbid or if you are ever laid off.

Education and Learning Effective Written Expression
Writing well requires practice, just like other things in life. The good news is that your talents will become better the more you practice. Effective written communication is crucial for both leadership and achieving goals. Making sure that instructions are understood and followed correctly may make all the difference between success and failure.

Whatever the project or activity, a competent leader must communicate their objectives and future vision. Since nobody can read minds, communication is necessary for more complex undertakings so that everything gets completed.

Make it clear what you desire. Consider the queries that readers may have. Bring together all the resources your audience will need to do a job, then assist them as they work on it. Tell your employees how you would want to be contacted. Go above and above by carefully reviewing each email you send out. Take your time.

After that, proofread everything at least one more time using your grammar and spelling checker before pressing the Send key. Give instructions as appropriate, but don't micromanage your employees let them make decisions on their own. The outcome may surprise you in a good way.

Pay Attention to What You Say

Words have influence. Take a look at any compelling newspaper editorial or a few of the most well-known historical speeches ever made. Communicate your true feelings and intentions. It's not necessary to sound like a dictionary and use flowery language. To ensure that everyone who reads what you have written can comprehend it, be concise and clear. Thesaurus use for synonym discovery is recommended. Look up any unfamiliar terms in the dictionary.

Keep an eye on your paragraphs

For corporate writing as well as digital communications like emails, websites, and PowerPoint presentations, short, snappy paragraphs are ideal. Writing drawn-out college essays is not necessary to make your argument. It may not always be easy to teach leadership skills and effective communication techniques, but the rewards may be substantial if you can operate a more productive business with better communications that your employees will read, that educate them, and that guarantee everyone is on the same page.

There will always be leaders and followers, according to some, and some individuals are just born leaders. Even if they may have a strong personality and a desire to lead, it will require a certain sort of individual to persuade others to follow them. Usually, they will do this by setting an example for others to follow and demonstrating to them how things should be done.

Effective communication may be shown by a competent leader that prioritizes it in all of their written, phone, and in-person contacts. In your leadership capacity, evaluate your communication skills and look for areas where you may grow. You may go even further on the path to becoming a successful leader in this manner. I hope you get the greatest possible outcome!

CHAPTER 5:

INTRODUCTION TO EFFECTIVE COMMUNICATION

The foundation of successful relationships is effective communication, which promotes comprehension and cooperation. It entails speaking with clarity, paying attention, and modifying communication methods to appeal to a range of listeners. Gaining proficiency in this area can help you establish solid connections on a personal and professional level by ensuring that relevant and accurate information is shared.

Verbal and nonverbal communication are the two forms of communication. These two are significant since they complement one another.

1. IMPORTANCE OF VERBAL COMMUNICATION
2. NON VERBAL COMMUNICATION IS ALSO AN INTEGRAL PART OF EXPRESSING YOURSELF

IMPORTANCE OF VERBAL COMMUNICATION
In the complex web of interpersonal relationships, verbal communication acts as a pivot, creating bonds of comprehension, expression, and connection. Words have a great role in interpersonal interactions; they are more than just a means of exchanging information. Its importance strikes a

deep chord, impacting social, professional, and personal dynamics.

Fundamentally, verbal communication serves as a medium for the resonance of ideas, thoughts, and feelings. People are able to communicate deeply felt emotions, share experiences, and explain difficult ideas because of the richness of language. When it comes to intimate and empathetic relationships, good verbal communication acts as the glue that holds people together. Clear and nuanced communication of ideas creates a common understanding that goes beyond surface-level encounters and paves the way for deeper relationships.

Effective verbal communication is essential for success in the workplace. Said words have an impact on results and company culture in anything from boardroom discussions to team cooperation. Progress may be sparked by a team member's creative concept expression or a leader's ability to convey an inspiring vision. Not only does clear verbal communication reduce miscommunication, but it also boosts self-assurance and fosters teamwork and productivity.

Furthermore, verbal communication is dynamic by nature, adjusting to the subtleties of various circumstances and audiences. Depending on the tone, pitch, and word choice used, the same message may have various resonances with different people. Not only does the ability of audience-tailored communication improve persuasiveness, but it also fosters inclusion. Effective verbal communication may help people negotiate different viewpoints, cross cultural divides, and foster an atmosphere of respect for one another.

Verbal communication has a significant influence on public discourse and collective awareness within a larger cultural environment. Political speakers, for example, use language as a tool for persuasion to influence people's beliefs and energize audiences. Effective communicators, or public speakers, may mobilize people to support causes and start conversations about important topics.

In summary, it is impossible to overestimate the value of verbal communication. It is essential to human connection, a driving force behind both professional and personal development, and a significant influence in forming societal norms. People who are proficient in articulation, active listening, and flexibility may unleash the transforming power of spoken language and effectively negotiate the complex terrain of interpersonal communication.

NON VERBAL COMMUNICATION IS ALSO AN INTEGRAL PART OF EXPRESSING YOURSELF

Unnoticed in its complexity, nonverbal communication is a complex and essential part of self-expression. In addition to the words we say, our body language, facial expressions, gestures, and even the tone of our voice all contribute to the message we want others to understand. This unspoken language permeates daily encounters and is vital to how other people understand and react to our emotions.

One of the main components of nonverbal communication is facial expression, which provides insight into our feelings. A grin may communicate warmth and approachability across cultural divides, but a wrinkled brow might suggest uncertainty or worry. With its wide range of expressions, the face serves as a canvas for our deepest emotions, giving our spoken words more nuance and genuineness.

Similar to this, our body language shapes the story of our conversation like a silent choreographer. Our posture, seating arrangement, and gait all convey a great deal about our self-assurance, curiosity, and involvement. An assured gait or an open body might highlight the certainty in our speech, yet fidgeting or crossing one's arms could unintentionally convey discomfort or defensiveness. Comprehending and using body language enables people to harmonize their nonverbal indicators with their spoken words, creating a congruence that amplifies the communication's overall effect.

Another aspect of non-verbal communication is the tone and pitch of our voice, which conveys emotions. A hard and aggressive pitch may highlight conviction, while a gentle, comforting tone might suggest empathy. Our voice modulation adds layers of significance to our words, affecting how others hear and understand what we're saying. Misunderstandings may result from a mismatch between vocal expression and verbal substance, underscoring the need to pay attention to this often disregarded component of communication.

Beyond these specifics, gestures create a silent conversation that enhances and supports spoken communication. Language limitations may be overcome by a handshake, a nod of agreement, or a wave of welcome to establish rapport and communicate understanding. Communication breakdowns may result from the lack or misunderstanding of these non-verbal clues, underscoring the importance of understanding the function gestures play in expressing feelings that are not expressed.

Nonverbal communication is essentially like an unseen thread that weaves through our spoken words to form a whole expressive tapestry. It is more than just an addition to spoken communication; rather, it is a complex dance that sometimes supports and sometimes contradicts the overt substance of our statements. Gaining an understanding of non-verbal signals enables people to establish rapport, communicate authentically, and skillfully handle the nuances of interpersonal communication. Both verbal and nonverbal components work together in the great symphony of self-expression to provide a more complex and meaningful communication experience.

CHAPTER 6:

IMPORTANCE OF EFFECTIVE COMMUNICATION

Success in a variety of spheres of life, such as the workplace, personal connections, and social cohesion, depends on effective communication. It involves communicating ideas in a clear, succinct, and impactful way that goes beyond just sharing data. It encourages teamwork and productivity in a work setting. It fosters closeness and trust in partnerships. It encourages tolerance and cross-cultural communication in society.

Additionally essential to personal growth is effective communication, which promotes self-expression and ongoing education. Its efficiency is influenced by both verbal and nonverbal clues, which makes it a crucial ability for negotiating the intricacies of interpersonal communication. "A Careless talk costs lives," goes a British propaganda line from World War II. Although this may come out as a little theatrical, the truth is that you will suffer the consequences in both scenarios if you are unable to adequately explain or deliver your idea.

Now, this loss might be of any kind—money, property, or even human life. Both our social and personal life will be negatively impacted by poor and ineffective communication. You must understand that there should be mental concord between the sender and the recipient if you want communication to become more successful. A communication breakdown will develop and the result of the conversation will not be particularly helpful if the sender is communicating in one mental frame while the recipient is in another.

Enhancing your mood may also help you communicate more effectively and concretely, since a negative gesture might convey the incorrect message and lead others to interpret you negatively. Conversely, a good attitude can make the communication process as a whole pleasant.

In every corporate setting, communication skills are crucial, and good or poor communication may either advance or hinder an organization's success. Just because certain grammatical errors are repaired doesn't mean that communication in an organization is now flawless. Rather, communication is something that requires your continuous attention, upkeep, and progress.

Make sure the person you are speaking with understands what you are saying while you are having an interpersonal conversation. It won't be enough to just ask, "Do you know what I mean?" at the conclusion.

EFFECTIVE COMMUNICATION DAMAGE

You may always create a map showing the benefits and drawbacks of both good and bad communication. It won't take you long to realize that poor communication may cost you dearly in terms of work, time, production, advancement, and other related aspects.

You will have to start the report again from the beginning if you miscommunicate with your supervisor about a particular report. This will take time and effort, and most of the time, poor communication will make you feel embarrassed. Finding misunderstanding as soon as possible is the greatest course of action since the sooner it is found, the sooner it can be fixed. Ineffective communication can also make you feel a lot more stressed and tense since, should you skip work due to it, your supervisor will be upset with you and it's possible that some of your coworkers may get upset as well. Thus, it may cause disruptions to your whole workspace. You must communicate well if you want to avoid all of the aforementioned issues.

CHAPTER 7:

7CS OF EFFECTIVE COMMUNICATION

1.} COMPLETENESS WILL BRING THE DESIRED RESPONSE

2.} CONCISENESS WILL SAVE TIME

3.} CONSIDERATION MEANS UNDERSTANDING OF HUMAN NATURE

4.} CONCRETENESS REINFORCES CONFIDENCE

5.} CLARITY CAN MAKE THINGS MORE COMPREHENSIVE

6.} COURTESY MAKES RELATIONS STRONGER

7.}CORRECTNESS WILL AVOID ALL THE CONFUSION.

There are seven key components that may turn an average conversation into a very productive one. I will go over each of these seven Cs of communication in this chapter.

1.} COMPLETENESS WILL BRING THE DESIRED RESPONSE

Completeness refers to the idea that everything you say in a speech should be true and comprehensive, with no information left out. People often make the assumption that listeners or the audience are aware of certain facts. This is not the best course of action since you won't be able to provide all the specifics of the main goal if you begin to assume this first.

The whole concept will get muddled, and you'll have difficulty explaining it to others. In order to make your ideas more understandable, you should strive to provide some more information in addition to the extensive details you give your audience. Make sure you are addressing every question your subject may raise as you are putting up your report or presentation.

The audience will ask you more reasonable questions and will have a better comprehension of your subject as a result. It often occurs that someone will ask you, "What are you actually trying to say?" once your presentation at work is over. After a long presentation, this is perhaps the worst thing someone can say to you, but you should reconsider why they said it. Your presentation will have some shortcomings, or there may be some unclear elements that have compelled that individual to say so.

You should make an effort to make your presentation more comprehensive and precise, covering even the smallest details and not disregarding any facts, in order to steer away from such awkward circumstances. Completeness elicits the intended reaction from the audience, listener, or receiver. You must include whatever you believe relevant to your discussion subject and make an effort to explain both constructive and destructive methods.

2.} CONCISENESS WILL SAVE TIME

Another crucial component of good communication is conciseness. This is particularly true when discussing corporate communication, in which case you should know that being succinct will make your message more appropriate, direct, and easy to comprehend. In today's world, time is of the essence. You may convey the same ideas and have the same conversation for thirty minutes, but nobody has the time to listen to you for an hour.

Furthermore, your audience will get disinterested and choose to either exit the conversation or cease paying attention if you lengthen the time by adding needless pauses, repeating content, and using other similar strategies. You should refrain from adding extraneous material and limit your inclusion of pertinent details regarding your subject. If you are presenting your organization's yearly budget, for instance, you should stick to the subject and refrain from including extraneous examples of how to increase or decrease the budget.

Presenting an annual budget report is your goal; adding recommendations that are related to someone else is not appropriate. If you attempted to overexpress yourself, it may happen that your audience would get confused by your flowery words and that there would be a great deal of debate that they would never be able to grasp. Thus, be succinct in your information and save both yourself and your audience time.

3.} CONSIDERATION MEANS UNDERSTANDING OF HUMAN
NATURE

One of the most crucial components of good communication is consideration, which will ensure that you have a deeper understanding of the other person. Saying "consider then" implies that you should give certain things more thought and make sure your message is always delivered in an upbeat manner. Try to overcome any unfavorable aspects in your debate by focusing on the good ones, even if there are several.

It's critical to recognize that the more advantages you mention and the more you can explain about them, the more engaging the conversation will be. In order to increase attention and pique people's interest in incorporating the benefits of your talk into their daily lives, you should make an effort to thoroughly describe each and every one of its advantages.

Try concentrating more on "you" as opposed to "I" or "We." Additionally, it conveys the extremely positive message that you really care more about other people than about yourself. The portion of contemplation is finished with the proverb "Think before you speak." Everything should be thoroughly examined before being shared with others. Consider all aspects from the perspective of the recipient, since this will help you consider concerns that are sometimes overlooked when focusing on a single strategy.

Negative phrases like "I hate" should never be used; instead, use "I prefer." Likewise, there are a plethora of substitutes you may choose from to steer clear of all the toxicity in your conversation. If you must say confident, you may also say unstoppable. Similarly, blessed can be used in lieu of lucky since all words have the same good connotation, but the alternatives are far better.

4.} CONCRETENESS REINFORCES CONFIDENCE

To be concrete, the facts and numbers that you give in your debate should be precise and correct.

The information should be very clear, and accuracy is even more crucial since people tend to value words especially those that pertain to the numbers you represent.

Additionally, your choice of verbs should be very specific and vivid, and the way you phrase it should provide a favorable impression of your subject as a whole. People will start to feel confused and think badly if you start to seem a bit hazy, ambiguous, and generic about the facts. A single point of emphasis will be removed, which will make communication less effective.

Providing reliable and accurate data and statistics will inevitably increase your self-assurance. You should make an effort to compile data from various polls, and the internet may be a great resource for doing this kind of research. Whatever subject you have, you can locate content in all forms that is relevant to it. You may ask folks about their thoughts on your subject and then watch to see how your audience reacts. However, keep in mind that all of the data should be precise, pertinent to your main idea, and free of unnecessary information.

5.} CLARITY CAN MAKE THINGS MORE COMPREHENSIVE

People tend to confuse clarity with only making a truth more obvious, but in reality, clarity is more about improving your voice and message in its whole. To effectively communicate your point, you must make more deliberate word choices and stick to plainer language. The audience will be able to understand your point of view more clearly and decipher your message more readily if your language is simpler.

The best technique to increase clarity is to use plainer language and write paragraphs that are easier to read and comprehend. Try to keep your approach informal and avoid using too many official terms. If you attempted to be too formal in your approach and used excessively sophisticated vocabulary, keep in mind that not everyone can grasp such language. People these days, in particular, have very poor language skills, and formal language is only used in news articles and newspaper columns.

Ordinary folks can grasp straightforward, everyday language, therefore that's the greatest approach to get your point across in its most unadulterated form. Clarity, as stated in the headline, makes your communication more complete. This is true because, if you use fewer words, the recipient will find it simpler to understand and decipher your message and grasp its exact meaning.

On the other hand, if you overcomplicate the message and use a lot of heavy words, you will only be able to communicate half of the meaning. The other half will be obscured by the heavy phrases. To ensure that everyone can comprehend your message, attempt to make it as plain as you can by using fewer, simpler terms.

6.} COURTESY MAKES RELATIONS STRONGER

Being courteous to the other person entails treating them with some respect. You should begin and conclude your letter with polite words and phrases, particularly when it comes to business communication. This is only a means of elevating the receiver's feelings.

You should carefully consider the words you use since they may convey civility. Always consider the audience's quality, and your obligation increases if you are presenting to your supervisor. Always speak in a nondiscriminatory manner to convey to the other person that you respect their opinions and will not discriminate against them. The other person will feel good about your conversation and become even more interested if you are being considerate, kind, grateful, and use polite language and gestures.

You may use the following straightforward example: if you get an email that begins with the words "hi" or "hello," you won't appreciate it very much. However, if the email also says "hi our respectful and valued customer," you will most likely attempt to check into it. These are a few examples of ways individuals demonstrate their professionalism.

7.} CORRECTNESS WILL AVOID ALL THE CONFUSION

You must target the appropriate audience if you want to be proper, and awareness necessitates correctness. It is important to understand the reader's or audience's social, educational, and religious background before tailoring your language to suit them. A CEO will begin to feel confused if you start talking to labor in the same manner that you talk to them.

This does not imply that you should not treat laborers with the same respect as you do the CEO; rather, it indicates that you should treat them with distinct standards of decency and adhere to certain guidelines. You should also use appropriate language, prevent punctuation mistakes, and provide exact and correct information. Your communication will be more accurate and efficient with all of these features.

People won't respect your message if you start using unclear or unsuitable language, or if you make too many punctuation and grammatical errors. In the end, it will be noted as inefficient communication. However, you may quickly fix this by including some accurate data and statistics and maintaining clear, proper syntax.

These are the seven Cs of communication, and if you can master them all, your communication style will be very successful. To put it simply, a communication is regarded as successful if it is coherent, thorough, thoughtful, accurate, polite, and concrete.

CHAPTER 8:

WHAT IS EFFECTIVE COMMUNICATION IN A GOOD LEADER

While some individuals appear to be destined for leadership roles, others are forced into them. History demonstrates how several individuals with quite modest beginnings have unexpectedly become legendary both in their own day and later on. What makes a Napoleon or a Julius Caesar? What makes someone like Warren Buffett, Steve Jobs, and Richard Branson possible in this day and age, when there is less conquest involved?

They are all skilled communicators some may even refer to them as "spin doctors" which is the one thing they have in common. They know how important it is to provide a vision that people want to be a part of. Both Napoleon and Julius Caesar were skilled at using propaganda to persuade people that their setbacks were really wins.

Proficient contemporary executives like Branson and Jobs established businesses from the ground up, ensuring that each employee understood the significance of the goal and was prepared to contribute in some way. Every chance for leadership will not only bring about triumphs but also provide challenges, traps, and difficult times. A great leader may be identified by their response to these trying times and to the many people who want to tear them down.

Time is also of the essence, as it is with many things in life. It might be challenging to learn how to speak successfully to your target audience at the appropriate time and location, but doing so can have a lot of advantages.

Recognize Your Audience

Understanding your audience is the most crucial component of any good communication. Since this audience will be diverse, it is essential for leaders to possess the talent of adaptability in their communication approaches. In the course of a typical day, as the head of an organization or division, you may talk to:

- Workers
- Shareholders
- Business associates
- Potential business associates
- Suppliers Clients
- Kids exploring your facilities... and more.

The secret to effective communication is in how you talk to them and what you decide to say or not say. You wouldn't discuss your Q4 sales figures with the kids, for instance. Additionally, you would only provide departmental evaluations to your employees rather than your clients.

The Appropriate Moment

Another crucial factor is timing. For instance, although no company leader enjoys breaking bad news, there are situations when things might become worse the more you try to avoid it. In the event that a downturn forces you to begin firing employees, you should notify them as quickly as possible.

The Appropriate Look

By using the example of needing to break terrible news, you also need to decide on the appropriate time and mode of communication. Should you keep your mouth shut around those who are being given the cold shoulder? Send emails to all of them? Or is it better to send out an email to arrange a time for this crucial meeting? How do you break the news while everyone is in the meeting? Do you just state unequivocally that layoffs will occur and stop there? Or will you outline the rationale for the choice, the actions that will come next, and your predictions for the future?

Speaking is not the only crucial leadership skill, listening is also vital. Will you allow employees to raise questions on the overall situation and the redundancies? or let your supervisors handle it? Following the meeting, you will have many choices and follow-up procedures to choose from. Will you give the pink slip to each employee or will your hiring manager do it on their behalf? Or would these employees only get notice and receive no acknowledgement or gratitude for all of their previous work?

Sometimes speaking nothing at all may be a beneficial form of communication, depending on the situation. When an employee receives a pink slip without explanation or gratitude, they are likely to be much more irate than when they are treated like human beings.

What You Say and Don't Say Counts

However, providing excessive details might put you in legal hot water if the employee feels that they were let go because you "don't like them" or that you are engaging in discriminatory behavior. Allegations of ageism, sexism, racism, and other types of discrimination may harm your business and perhaps have a negative financial impact.

As a result, it's critical that managers and employees understand how you as the leader speak to each and every one of your employees. It is important to always oppose offensive humor, bullying, and aggressive behavior in all contexts, including emails, social media, and in-person interactions among coworkers. To others, even "harmless teasing" may be cruel and seen as bullying.

Continuation

Follow-up is crucial in determining if something vital is communicated successfully or not. Referring back to the layoff scenario from earlier, it will be crucial to call another meeting to discuss what comes next for the employees who are left behind after the layoffs. Meetings will also be necessary to ensure that, with their departure, all of the tasks performed by the laid-off employees are covered.

Being Observed

Even the most capable executives want to just hide in their offices when things become hard. However, being apparent is often among the most effective ways to lead. An open-door policy that gives individuals the impression that they may approach you with queries and issues and that you'll take them seriously and treat them with respect can also be beneficial.

Establishing the Tone

Oftentimes, the most crucial part of leading is setting the tone. A leader that exudes positivity and a can-do attitude is more likely to attract followers than someone who conveys negativity all the time. Strong communication abilities enable a leader to reinterpret negative situations in a manner that keeps their followers engaged.

For instance, it should be made apparent that short-term losses are being made in order to achieve long-term benefits when it comes to layoffs. In the event that two departments join, a competent leader would outline all of the advantages and suggest ways to increase productivity.

Communicating Change

A lot of individuals detest change. People get so used to their routines that any change may be very unpleasant and can seem to be a severe danger to life as they know it, despite the fact that this is an inevitable reality of existence. Although this won't always be the case, showing empathy for this viewpoint may make the adjustments easier.

Organizing Frequent Meetings

Frequent meetings provide an opportunity for transparent communication and feedback. Don't hold meetings merely for the purpose of holding them. Clearly state the purpose of each meeting, as well as any agenda items and next actions. As soon as possible, follow up on any action items that came up during these discussions.

Having Effective Listening Skills

Many people think that having a strong voice is the only thing that makes a successful leader. The reality is that a good leader listens as well. Rather than believing they already know everything, they are empathetic, respect other people's perspectives, and are lifelong learners. Recognize that humans are only human. Everyone is prone to error. Investigate the causes of any mistakes that were committed.

Pay attention and express your opinions. Look for concepts and breakthroughs. If you believe someone deserves another opportunity, give them one. Consider your coworkers like you would your finest supervisor. Although we will never be able to put ourselves in another person's shoes, we may attempt to be more patient and sympathetic when they are going through personal or professional difficulties so that everyone feels appreciated.

Never Make Assumptions

Communicate clearly both orally and in writing at all times. Any critical information should be confirmed in writing, including emails, such as following up on a phone call or team meeting. Particularly when any deadlines are near, be sure to double-check everything. It is preferable to repeat yourself and provide a succinct summary of pertinent dates and points in your messages.

Assume, for instance, that everyone is already knowledgeable when in fact they may not be.If you are a corporate leader, these are some of the most crucial elements of successful communication. Depending on whether the message is verbal or written, your strategy will change somewhat. Let's examine verbal communication in the next part.

CHAPTER 9:

ORAL COMMUNICATION STRATEGIES

The majority of people are aware of the long-standing connection between effective oral communication and commercial success. Both big and small businesses recognize the value of effective oral communication and work to develop this talent whenever they can. The benefits of possessing strong and efficient oral communication abilities will be emphasized even more by the following points:

When meeting new clients and consumers, presentations are often the first media utilized. When a presenter has strong oral communication abilities, they can convey the required content in an engaging way that exudes expertise. The presenter's strong oral communication abilities are likely to persuade and allure most listeners, therefore this professionalism impression will guarantee that little to no disagreement is made about the delivered content.

In the customer engagement phase, oral communication is also a crucial component that is required. This pivotal phase essentially solidifies whatever potential future the firm may have with the other party. The oral communication's role would be the primary contributing factor if the conversation proceeds well and the customer is persuaded and satisfied. Both online and offline corporate organizations need spoken communication during interoffice interactions.

This includes all of the many layers of information that must be shared in order to keep the organization operating efficiently. Even with some distinguishing characteristics, including the different staff levels engaged, oral communication is still seen to be the most efficient way to transmit and receive information. Additionally, oral communication gives the material being provided a more intimate personal connection. Other than word choice used in the written content, there is no true connecting emotion that can be assessed with the other electronically recorded information delivery.

CHAPTER 10:

WRITTEN COMMUNICATION TECHNIQUES

All entrepreneurs should endeavor to become proficient in written communication skills or at least equip themselves with them. It is impossible to ignore the widespread usage of this medium for communication in favor of other channels.

Knowing how successful written communication is can motivate the owner of the company to make sure every written correspondence is well-prepared and has a purpose. A few benefits of developing strong written communication abilities are as follows:

There are a few important considerations to make while using textual communication approaches. First and foremost, clarity is essential. Make sure your message is clear by keeping your language basic and structuring your ideas rationally. Steer clear of technical phrases or jargon that might be confusing to your audience.

Think about your audience second. Adjust your writing style to the right amount of formality and tone of voice for the given context. For instance, you should use a more serious tone while sending a business email, but you may be more informal and conversational when writing a message to a friend.

Next, make sure your writing is organized well. Begin with a concise introduction that highlights the key ideas you'll be covering and draws the reader in. To divide up your thoughts and make your writing easier to read, use paragraphs. Every paragraph need to concentrate on a particular subject or notion.

Don't forget to check your spelling, grammar, and punctuation. Check your work for mistakes or typos that can cast doubt on your reliability. Employing appropriate language and punctuation indicates that you take writing seriously and improves the effectiveness of your message.

Finally, pay attention to your tone. The way you write has a big influence on how others understand what you're trying to say. Make appropriate word and sentence structure choices based on the tone you want to convey—either informal, professional, persuasive, or educational.

Never forget that practice makes perfect! You will improve at refining your written communication skills the more you write. Please get in touch if you ever need help getting your work proofread or if you need feedback.

Written communication is a good way to illustrate the element of clarity because it can be used as legally binding documents in many serious situations.

Clear requirements and agreed-upon principles are spelled out in written communication, which facilitates the organizational engine's smoother operation.

Another benefit of written communication is that it can be used to create something relatively permanent, which is helpful for keeping records and documenting information.

This is a valuable resource in the business world that can be used as a point of reference or for clarification.

Because everything is recorded and readily accessible for review, this kind of communication also facilitates the appropriate distribution of duties in an unambiguous and transparent manner.

Conveniently, it also removes the chance of misunderstandings and poor communication, though these things do happen occasionally but not very often.

The presentation of the information includes elements of definition, precision, and explicitness, which helps to maintain and improve the organization's image.

There aren't many other venues that, from a legal perspective, may provide uncontested material that can be used as a defining element in a potential dispute.

Every business entity should make it a point to have written documentation supporting all forms of communication to make sure unfavorable things never put the company in danger.

CHAPTER 11:

TYPES OF PERSONALITIES

The four personality types' evolutionary history, often known as... Hippocrates was the first of the four temperaments to emerge 24 centuries ago. He referred to the four personalities as blood, phlegm, yellow bile, and black bile. What role do personality types play in these fluids, then?

Hippocrates defined these liquids as symbolic of an individual's state of health.
- Black bile = Melancholy
- Yellow bile = Choleric,
- Phlegm = Phlegmatic
- Blood = Sanguine.

These days, there are four personality types: phlegmatic, sanguine, choleric, and melancholy

Let's take a closer look at the intriguing realm of personality types and how it all started about 2400 years ago with Hippocrates.

Hippocrates, who is often called the "father of medicine," created the Four Humors hypothesis. He thought that blood, yellow bile, black bile, and phlegm were the four main fluids, or humors, that make up the human body. Hippocrates believed that an imbalance of these humors would lead to distinct behaviors and personality characteristics.

According to the Four Humors hypothesis, a person's prevailing humor may be used to categorize them into one of four primary personality types. These personality types were called sanguine (related to blood), choleric (related to yellow bile), melancholy (related to black bile), and phlegmatic (related to phlegm) based on the matching humor.

It was often thought that people with sanguine personalities were upbeat, gregarious, and outgoing. They were seen as upbeat, vivacious people who delighted in social situations.

The traits of the choleric personality type were drive, ambition, and assertiveness. They were regarded as naturally gifted leaders who were very well-organized and goal-oriented.

The melancholy personality type was linked to contemplation, sensitivity, and introversion. They were seen as thoughtful people who often showed intense feelings and were inclined toward contemplation.

Phlegmatic personality types are characterized as relaxed, peaceful, and easygoing. They were regarded as trustworthy, patient, and excellent listeners.

The basis for understanding personality types was established by the Four Humors hypothesis, although contemporary psychology has advanced much since then. Modern theories of personality, such the Myers-Briggs Type Indicator (MBTI), the

Enneagram, and the Big Five (OCEAN) model, have surfaced to provide more thorough and intricate frameworks for understanding personality.

These more recent theories provide a more thorough and precise explanation of individual variations by accounting for a larger variety of personality characteristics and dimensions. Among other things, they take into account traits like agreeableness, conscientiousness, extraversion, openness to new experiences, and emotional stability.

In order to have a greater understanding of ourselves and others, it is crucial to delve into the richness of information and study that has been generated throughout the years, even if we may recognize the roots of personality typing with Hippocrates and the Four Humors.

Each personality type has unique advantages and disadvantages. Although everyone of us has traits from all four types, we all have a strong and a less dominant personality type.

- Being melancholic indicates a high level of analysis.
- To be choleric is to aspire to perpetual dominance.
- Being phlegmatic denotes a nurturing nature.
- Sanguine just indicates you want to enjoy yourself.

Another name for melancholy is an Emerald, Green, or Conscientious. This personality type is analytical, planner, inventive, analytical, accurate, meticulous, organized, philosophical, perfectionist, economical, idealistic, and goal-oriented. Introverted, easily depressed, overly cautious, prone to analysis paralysis, laid back, skeptical, and pessimistic are the traits of this personality that it lacks.

persons who are close to Melancholy persons should refrain from using generalizations in their speech. Phrases like "never" and "always" will not be respected. Reduce the loudness of your voice and maintain a pleasant tone if at all feasible. If you show them your negativity while you're in a foul mood, they'll take it personally and wonder what went wrong all day. Details are necessary in order to persuade melancholies. They want access to all of the PowerPoint's points and an explanation of each one, along with any additional in-depth information. You may want to provide them a lot of detail-rich extra content.

Choleric, also known as Dominance, Ruby, or Red. This personality type is driven by its innate qualities as a leader—it is goal-oriented, ambitious, gregarious, optimistic, hardworking, aggressive, strong-willed, decisive, confident, independent, successful, risk-taking, and direct. Domineering, My Way Or The High Way, Rule Breaker, Compulsive, Controlling, Cold, Tactless, Intolerant, Indifferent, Bossy, and Impatient are some of this personality's shortcomings.

The shortcomings of a choleric include hostility and violence. The most probable person to have a volatile temper is a choleric; they are horn blowers and door slammers who may harbor resentment for a very long period. This involves a tongue that is sharp and caustic, and the choleric will seldom hold back while reprimanding someone. You must earn the respect of chocerics in order to persuade them. You lose if they think you're unsure or unprepared.

They enjoy champions. Telling the cholerics that all the leaders will be there can help you persuade them to go to the event. Explain to them how your assistance will improve their leadership skills. Leaders who are clerics do so by virtue of their character.

Phlegmatic—also referred to as Yellow, Steadiness, and Pearl. This personality type is characterized by its ability to care for others, be stable, patient, attentive, peaceful, tolerant, laid-back, calm, dependable, loyal, pleasant, inoffensive, nurturing, and sympathetic. This personality's shortcomings include being unsure of themselves, being afraid of being rejected, being permissive, worrying, shy, bashful, nonchalant, timid, loner, fearful, hesitant, and compromising.

"Easy going" is a better description of the phlegmatic. He is a calm, stable individual who does not get easily upset. He has the most agreeable disposition of any kind. He leads a contented, peaceful, and unexcited life. The most erratic temperament type is the phlegmatic, despite their laid-back demeanor. He often uses comedy to illustrate his arguments.

The phlegmatic stays out of other people's affairs and is more of an observer. A phlegmatic must be persuaded that something is in the group's best interests. It is often necessary to ask them for their opinion in a format. It could be necessary for you to speak with them in a manner that maintains equality and prevents them from feeling in control. They take the lead by cooperating.

Sanguine, also known as Blue, Topaz, and Influence. This personality type excels in being joyful, sincere, apologetic, inspiring, enthusiastic, creative, optimistic, charismatic, entertaining, curious, giving back to the community, advocating, expressive, gregarious, and outgoing. Talkative, forgetful, a bad listener, repetitive, frantic, interruptive, erratic, nervous, disorganized, messy, moody, showy, changeable, and scatterbrained are some of this personality's shortcomings.

He finds comfort in the company of others and dislikes alone. He's often referred to as a "toucher" since he will reach out and touch the other person's shoulder or arm while they're speaking. More reserved temperaments might feel uneasy and uneasy about this. Tell a sanguine personality how much fun it will be or provide them a prominent spot in advance if you want them to attend an event. For an occasion, a sanguine would likely make an excellent master or mistress of ceremonies. Sanguines take the lead by using their charm.

CHAPTER 12:

BODY LANGUAGE BASICS

When we are in public, our body language that is, how we use various portions of our bodies tells a lot about how we are feeling emotionally. Experts have observed that just seeing someone's physical appearance may reveal a lot about their mental state. We refer to this as interpreting body language. You can't do this too plainly now. You will be branded as a leech if you gaze at someone's body!

Comprehending nonverbal cues is essential for proficient communication since it often discloses implicit emotions and ideas. Key takeaways on the fundamentals of body language include:

1. Facial Expressions: -Eye Contact: Maintaining eye contact shows assurance and focus, whilst averting it might suggest unease or deceit.
   -grins: Sincere grins show warmth and include the eyes, but fake smiles could not.

2. Gestures: -Open vs. Closed Posture: Open poses convey openness and receptivity, while crossed arms may imply discomfort or defensiveness.

-Hand movements: While crossed arms may imply defensiveness or disagreement, excessive hand motions may suggest excitement.

3. Posture: -Upright Posture: Being upright when sitting or standing conveys self-assurance and focus.

-Slouched Posture: A slouched or slumped posture might suggest a lack of enthusiasm or attention.

4. Proximity: -Personal Space: Although cultural norms on respect for personal space differ, violating someone's personal space may make them uncomfortable or defensive.

-Closeness: Leaning in might be seen as engagement or interest, while leaning back could be interpreted as disengagement.

5. Touch: -Positive Touch: A handshake or a pat on the back are examples of appropriate touch that may imply warmth and kinship.

-Negative contact: Tension or discomfort may result from unwanted or improper contact.

6. Eye Movements: -Pupil Dilation: While constricted pupils may convey pain or disagreement, dilated pupils may convey interest or attraction.

-Gaze Direction: Direct gaze indicates engagement, but looking away might imply distraction or discomfort.

7. Head Motions:

-Nodding: Nodding may be used to express understanding, encouragement, or agreement.

-Head Tilt: Curiousity or interest may be shown by tilting the head.

8. imitating: -Mimicking Movements: You may convey rapport and connection by gently imitating someone's posture or motions.

9. Voice Tone and Pitch: -Voice Tone: Variations in tone may highlight certain points or disclose feelings.
-Pitch: While lower tones may imply authority or serenity, higher tones might imply tension or enthusiasm.

10. Cultural Awareness: -Cultural Variances: Understanding body language accurately requires being aware of cultural subtleties since various cultures may perceive body language differently.

Gaining a better understanding of these fundamentals of body language improves interpersonal communication abilities, building stronger bonds and enabling more fruitful exchanges. It's crucial to remember that context and individual characteristics are major factors in effectively understanding body language. One may improve their ability to understand and utilize body language in a variety of social and professional contexts with consistent practice and observation.

But there are little cues that people often leave behind, and it just takes a moment to pick them up. You may, for instance, merely observe how someone holds their lips while speaking or how their eyes move as they listen to you. You might see how they hold their arms and legs and how they use their hands.

Each of these important body language cues exist. Reading these indications doesn't take long, but if you pay attention and know what to look for, they might reveal a lot to you.

There are several ways in which this may be really beneficial to you if you give it some thought. Imagine all the things you could accomplish if you had access to someone else's mental state. In only a moment, you'll be able to predict their thoughts and their reactions to you! By having the ability to read people's minds, you might potentially provide them with exactly what they want while making a business proposal, even before they express any concerns. You could make them feel comfortable. When your loved one is around you, you can allay their worries anytime they surface.

The ability to read body language covertly is a powerful tool for personal growth in and of itself. People will view you more highly if you can maintain everyone's satisfaction. That might give you a great deal of confidence. It could make you a better person someone who can be relied upon at all times.

We're not claiming that these methods for interpreting body language are perfect. As always, there are exceptions, and there will be times when you need to use your better judgment. Ultimately, however, they are indications that, for the most part, will be effective in the majority of your encounters with others. This is the way humans generally behave, and you'll need to know how to sort out the uncommon responses that could come your way.

In relation to personal growth, you are immediately improving yourself if you are able to understand others' body language. Since you are aware of how body language is read, you can control your own body language to convey the messages you choose. Could that not be completed? Of course it could! You can undoubtedly enhance your own body language if you can read that of others.

CHAPTER 13:

THE IMPORTANCE OF BODY LANGUAGE

Beyond what we say in words, body language is a crucial component of communication. It's important for communicating our objectives, emotions, and ideas to other people. Let's take a closer look at the significance of body language.

First and foremost, one of the most effective nonverbal communication tools is body language. In reality, research indicates that nonverbal clues including posture, eye contact, gestures, and facial emotions account for a large amount of human communication. Since they may convey our genuine feelings and intentions, these nonverbal cues can have more power than words.

Accurately seeing and comprehending people is one of the main advantages of knowing how to read body language. We may learn a lot about someone's emotions, degree of participation, and general attitude by observing their body language. Open and relaxed body language, on the other hand, may show receptiveness and involvement. For instance, crossed arms and a closed-off posture may signal defensiveness or apathy.

Additionally, body language may improve the efficacy of our own communication. Being conscious of our own nonverbal signals helps us to better coordinate and persuade others by coordinating them with our spoken message. To strengthen the message we are attempting to get over, we may use nonverbal cues like standing tall, keeping eye contact, and making open movements.

Additionally important in establishing and maintaining connections is body language. It facilitates building rapport, trust, and connections with other people. We may establish a feeling of familiarity and empathy by mimicking and copying someone else's body language, such as their posture or gestures, which promotes deeper comprehension and better relationships.

Furthermore, body language may be useful in navigating cultural differences and social settings. Understanding how body language is interpreted and accepted in different cultures may help to avoid miscommunication and foster successful cross-cultural interactions.

It's important to remember that body language should be read in light of the circumstances and the unique characteristics of each person. While certain gestures or emotions may typically be interpreted in a certain way, it's important to take into account the individual's particular personality, cultural background, and any other pertinent information to avoid drawing hasty judgments.

Body language is an essential part of communication that may help us better understand others, communicate more effectively ourselves, and build deeper bonds with others. Through observing nonverbal indicators and being aware of our own body language, we may improve our communication skills and build deeper relationships with others around us.

The influence of body language is as powerful as spoken words, if not more so. In light of this, it's critical for those entering the corporate world to be conscious of their presentation. When attempting to leave an impression, keep the following in mind:

When standing, maintain your shoulders straight and your head high, and try to keep your back as straight as possible. It is intended for this attitude to convey a sense of firmness and confidence. It also indicates that the person is very relaxed and at peace with both the environment and himself.

Maintaining a sitting posture that is flattering to the person is crucial since nobody wants to be aware of their private matters. Maintaining an upright posture at all times conveys a sense of alertness and readiness to participate fully in the current circumstance. It's crucial to sit quietly since any movement will come off as uneasy or tense.

Hands: While most individuals wave or move their hands while speaking, this is not appropriate, particularly in a more formal context. It is common for hand motions to correspond with the level of excitement in a discussion; thus, it is important to notice and address this before someone feels uncomfortable.

Head movement: As long as it's not excessive, nodding at suitable intervals to indicate recognition or agreement is allowed. A person who bobbles their head excessively will thus be dismissed as a joke and not taken seriously.

The most revealing bodily movement is via facial expressions, which instantly convey to the other person what the person is thinking. Controlling one's facial emotions is a very valuable skill that must be developed.

Envision yourself sitting across from the interviewer at a job interview. They lean slightly forward, nod in agreement, and keep steady eye contact while you respond to their queries. Positive body language indicators like these show that the interviewer is attentive, interested, and open to your comments. This might help you feel more at ease and confident throughout the interview.

Let's now examine an other situation. During a chat with a friend, you see that they are tight, have crossed arms, and avoid making eye contact. These unfavorable body language indicators might indicate that your companion is feeling aloof or defensive. Understanding these cues enables you to modify your strategy and demonstrate empathy, for example, by enquiring as to whether everything is OK or extending assistance.

Body language conveys important information about the intentions, emotions, and ideas of the people involved in both cases. You may modify your communication style, establish rapport, and improve the general quality of your conversations by being mindful of these signs.

CHAPTER 14:

PUBLIC SPEAKING TIPS

The majority of businesspeople may at some time find themselves in a circumstance where giving a public speech is a requirement of their business relationship's advancement. A smaller number of individuals might also be the target audience for a public speech, so it's not always aimed at a broad one. The goal of the public speaking practice is to improve your ability to deliver information in an engaging and educational manner.

These are some pointers on what someone trying to practice public speaking should concentrate on:
A certain amount of conviction must permeate the overall delivery of the content while speaking in front of an audience. The quality that will connect with the recipient and pique their attention in the information being provided is this air of conviction. In addition to piqueing the listener's attention, a persuasive presentation will make them feel even more persuaded, which successfully guarantees the conversion to devoted clientele.

Giving a speech in public without using notes increases effectiveness. In addition to the risk that the content being read aloud won't be very interesting, there's also the risk that the presenter won't be able to engage the audience since they will be too preoccupied reading the information.

One of the most crucial things to focus on and make sure you practice all the time is maintaining eye contact. The presenter has very little chance of keeping the audience's attention for very long if they don't make the crucial eye contact. Maintaining eye contact is essential, even while presenting content that is interesting, since it allows the presenter to assess the audience's level of interest in the topic. This would enable the presenter to quickly make the required modifications to guarantee that the detrimental impact doesn't continue.

Many individuals find public speaking to be an intimidating experience, but with the correct strategies and tactics, you may develop into a confident and powerful orator. Here are some more ideas and pointers to help you become a better public speaker:

1. Prepare and Practice: Getting ready is one of the most crucial elements of public speaking. Spend some time thinking about your speech's framework, gathering information, and organizing your ideas. To guarantee a seamless delivery and to boost confidence, practice giving your speech many times.

2. Establish a Connection with Your Audience: Keep in mind that you are addressing a group of people, not simply a nameless assembly. By keeping eye contact, using realistic examples, and speaking in a conversational tone, you may build rapport with your audience. To maintain their interest, ask them questions, tell them tales, or include interactive components.

3. Use Visual Aids Wisely: Although they might improve your presentation, visual aids like slides or props should only be used judiciously and strategically. Make sure your images are clear, easy to understand, and pertinent to your primary ideas. They need to enhance rather than detract from your speech.

4. Master Your Body Language: How you present yourself may have a big influence on how others understand you. To accentuate important ideas, stand up straight, keep your posture correct, and make organic motions. Do not pace or fidget since these actions might be distracting. Always remember to smile and use your body language to convey confidence.

5. Master Your Voice: Be aware of the tone, tempo, and projection of your voice. Make sure that everyone in the audience can hear you well and loudly when you speak. To emphasize points, convey feelings, and maintain attention, change up the tempo and tone of your voice. To speak in a steady and composed tone, engage in breathing exercises.

6. Manage Your Nervousness: Feeling anxious before a public speech is common. Breathe deeply, see yourself succeeding, and concentrate on the point you want to make in order to calm yourself down. To establish momentum and capture the audience's interest, begin with a powerful start.

7. Practice Active Listening: Speaking in front of an audience is only one aspect of effective public speaking; the other is listening as well. Observe their responses, nonverbal clues, and

comments. Adapt your delivery to suit their level of interest and engagement.

8. Be Genuine and Enthusiastic: Your audience will connect with your genuineness and excitement. Talk from the heart, include anecdotes or personal experiences, and show how passionate you are about the topic. This will enable you to establish a stronger connection with your audience.

9. Managing Errors with Grace: It's critical to manage errors with grace when they occur. Don't freak out if you fumble your words or make a mistake. Breathe deeply, smile, and go on with assurance. Recall that most of the time, your audience understands you and values your sincerity. Accept any errors as teaching moments, and use what you've learned to your next public speaking events. You'll quickly develop into a confident and competent public speaker if you continue to practice and hone your abilities!

CHAPTER 15:

IMPROVING INTERPERSONAL COMMUNICATION SKILLS

1. ADAPTING TO CHANGE EASILY
2. TIMING IS CRUCIAL.

These days, everything and everyone thinks and performs extremely professionally since we live in such a high-tech society. You must possess great interpersonal communication skills if you are really interested in pursuing a job in one of the many flourishing firms. While some individuals are naturally gifted communicators and presenters, others, despite their greater competence and education, find it difficult to get their point across.

With the ability to captivate others with your ideas and word choice, these talents may assist you in reaching the highest levels of success in your life.

Two of the best tools for blazing a clear and direct path for yourself are your tongue and your intellect. If you have good interpersonal communication abilities, you can persuade others to do even the silliest things. You may become proficient in a variety of tactics that can help your communication abilities stand out.

I'll share some of the trade secrets for these communication abilities with you in this chapter so you may master them and take the world by storm.

ADAPTING TO CHANGE EASILY

If you are employed by a company, you may sometimes notice changes in the organizational culture. Whatever changes your organization is implementing, your interpersonal skills will improve greatly if you can accept them with ease. These changes could include technological advancements, a shift in the types of people joining, or the use of different performance-enhancing strategies.

These days, the majority of technical developments occur in organizations that are relatively simple to embrace with just a little amount of study. Your status will increase and other employees will begin to appreciate you more if you are the one to implement that change swiftly and successfully.

TIMING IS CRUCIAL

As I have stated in the previous chapter, time lost as a result of poor communication is extremely important because most modern organizations operate under extremely strict deadlines. If you are unable to meet these deadlines and manage your busy schedule, you will encounter many challenges. However, these issues can be resolved with enhanced interpersonal skills and effective time management.

Your ability to speak clearly and finish everything on your first try will boost your organization hype in addition to your interpersonal abilities. "Good communicators are made, not born," goes the proverb. If that's the case, you should never give up and put out your best effort to enhance your communication abilities, regardless of how poor your communication abilities have been in the past. Nobody can stop you from achieving your goal, and mastering these communication skills is also not that hard. To learn them, all you need is a little bravery and drive.

CHAPTER 16:

BECOMING A GOOD COMMUNICATOR FROM A GOOD COMMUNICATOR

It takes more than just linguistic proficiency to become an excellent communicator; one must also grasp the subtleties of successful interpersonal relations. Getting knowledge from someone who is an experienced communicator might provide insightful information. An effective communicator will often stress the need of active listening, or the capacity to understand not just what is being said but also the underlying feelings and intentions.

Effective communicators also excel at tailoring their message to the needs of their audience, understanding that precise and succinct communication is essential. An adept communicator knows when to talk and when to listen, and how to strike a balance between assertiveness and empathy. This subtle method promotes open communication by developing rapport and trust.

Nonverbal cues like tone and body language are crucial in communicating. Skilled communicators are aware of their nonverbal clues and how they affect the message as a whole. These little details, like as keeping eye contact and using the right gestures, add up to a thorough and consistent communication style.

The capacity to maintain composure under duress is another quality that skilled communicators often display. They endeavor to communicate with poise even in difficult circumstances because they recognize how important it is to control one's emotions. Their tenacity not only increases their credibility but also eases conversational tension.

Moreover, effective communicators always strive for personal development. They welcome criticism, actively seek it out, and are willing to improve their communication abilities. This dedication to self-improvement guarantees flexibility in a communication environment that is always changing.

To sum up, learning from a skilled communicator entails more than just picking up language skills; it also includes comprehending the nuances of successful communication. It involves developing active listening skills, being adept at nonverbal clues, adjusting to a variety of audiences, and adopting a development mentality. Acquiring these qualities may set one on the way to being an adept communicator who handles social situations with grace and efficiency.

Let's dive further on what gives us better illustration

1. COMMIT YOURSELF TO IMPROVE
2. TRAINING IS IMPORTANT
3. DEVELOPMENT SHOULD BE MONITORED.

There are a lot of people in your company that you will see, and you may believe, "They must have always been like this." However, this isn't the case for all of them since effective communication requires adhering to a set of norms. People you encounter may have these ideas so well ingrained in their lives that they no longer even consider them; instead, they just act on them. However, at some time in the past, they must have gone through the same stage that you are now going through. Thus, you must have the confidence to choose a direction.

There are several things you can do to improve your communication, and I will highlight a few of them in this conversation. As these statements make clear, interpersonal communication abilities are incredibly personal, yet they are all entirely learnt. Numerous tangible items may help you incorporate certain very successful interpersonal communication skills into your personality. All you have to do is prepare yourself and be willing to take on this challenge in order to better yourself overall.

COMMIT YOURSELF TO IMPROVE

You should dedicate yourself to mastering these talents, just like you would any other skill, and make sure that nothing is on your mind that may divert you from your goal. You may always work on your interpersonal skills to advance in your career if you can commit to something as specific as that. You will continue on the same road of advancement if you maintain your focus on the overall progress and benefit that this talent will provide you.

TRAINING IS IMPORTANT

Various training programs are available to enhance your interpersonal abilities. You may participate in these initiatives by signing up for online courses or making an effort to attend in-person sessions. Many people believe that taking these courses is only a means of generating money. If you believe that this is the case, you should seek for some free courses.

You may try your luck and develop your social skills by enrolling in one of the many free courses that are offered. They will provide you with some of the crucial and required instruction without charging you anything.

DEVELOPMENT SHOULD BE MONITORED

You have to keep an eye on your progress if you have been working to enhance your interpersonal communication abilities. You should attempt to compare yourself to others and determine the difference in order to improve and strengthen your talents. Seeking feedback from others is the most effective approach since it provides you with an accurate assessment of your communication abilities.

CHAPTER 17:

PROPERTIES OF INTERPERSONAL COMMUNICATION

1. INTERPERSONAL COMMUNICATION IS INESCAPABLE
2. INTERPERSONAL COMMUNICATION IS IRREVERSIBLE
3. INTERPERSONAL COMMUNICATION IS CONTEXTUAL

INTERPERSONAL COMMUNICATION IS INESCAPABLE

Even when you choose not to communicate, communication still occurs. You must make a gesture, which is a component of communication, to indicate that you do not want to converse. Another kind of communication is silence, and it varies throughout civilizations. In some cultures, pausing for a long time before responding to a question is considered dignified, while in others, it might be seen as foolish behavior.

This implies that verbal exchange is not the only form of communication. Conversely, there are situations when people may learn a lot from your body language. For instance, if your mother discovers you staying up late and doesn't say anything, you may tell from her emotions that she is conveying a "grounded" message.

INTERPERSONAL COMMUNICATION IS IRREVERSIBLE

Any kind of communication is irrevocable once it is said since words cannot be taken back. For this reason, the proverb "think before you speak" has gained popularity. Once you talk, you cannot undo the harm or advantage you have caused yourself.

There is another adage that goes, "Message will be heard in its most negative sense, if there is any," thus you need to make sure that you are using the most positive words and phrases to prevent any unwanted actions by your communication.This makes it quite evident that in order to communicate more effectively and positively, you should refrain from using derogatory language and idioms.

INTERPERSONAL COMMUNICATION IS CONTEXTUAL

You can never speak in solitude while using contextual communication; you always need someone to clarify what you've said. Anybody might be your life partner, a buddy, a social gathering, an organization, or anybody else, but you need someone to read and reply to your correspondence.

This makes it much more intriguing as it forces you to consider the other person's perspective more and adjust your communication appropriately when there is always a third party involved. You could have understood the message back then, but you might have communicated a different one if you had begun communicating in your own manner. One thing is clear from all of these qualities: you must communicate with extreme precision. If you omit any important details, the whole point of communication will be lost, and you will suffer some kind of loss.

CHAPTER 18:

IMPROVING SKILLS

In today's highly technologically advanced environment, everyone thinks and behaves in a very professional manner. Should you really want to pursue a job in one of the many rapidly expanding firms, you will need to possess great interpersonal communication abilities. While some people are naturally gifted communicators and presenters, others, despite their greater competence and education, find it difficult to get their point across.

With these abilities, you might achieve the most success in your life by captivating others with your ideas and language. One of your most incisive tools for paving a clear and direct path is your tongue, together with your intellect. If you have good interpersonal communication abilities, you can persuade others to do even the silliest things. You may acquire a variety of tactics that can really help your communication abilities stand out.

If you are employed by a company, you may sometimes notice changes in the organizational culture. Whatever changes your organization is implementing, your interpersonal skills will benefit greatly if you can accept them with ease. These changes could include technological advancements, a shift in the types of people joining, or the use of various performance-enhancing techniques.

These days, the majority of technological improvements occur in businesses that are quite simple to embrace with just a little investigation. If you're the one who makes that adjustment quickly and successfully, other employees will start to appreciate you more and your status will increase.

The amount of time lost as a result of poor communication is particularly important because most modern businesses operate under strict deadlines. If you are unable to meet these deadlines while maintaining a busy schedule, you will encounter numerous difficulties. However, this problem can be resolved with better interpersonal skills and effective time management. In addition to improving your interpersonal abilities, being able to speak effectively and finishing everything on your first try will also make you more valuable to the company.

Similar to the well-known proverb "great communicators are made, not born," If that's the case, you should never give up and should make every attempt to improve your communication abilities, no matter how poor a communicator you have been in the past. Nobody can stop you from achieving your goal, and mastering these communication skills is also not that tough. To learn them, all you need is a little bravery and drive.

CHAPTER 19:

HOW BAD COMMUNICATION DAMAGES YOUR BUSINESS

Success in the ever-changing corporate world depends on having excellent communication. On the other hand, inadequate communication may do serious harm to your company, affecting all aspects and impeding expansion. A breakdown in collaboration is one of the most noticeable effects right away. Team members may find it difficult to comprehend their responsibilities, the company's overarching vision, and their own roles when communication routes are compromised.

Errors, delays, and a lack of cohesiveness among staff members are all consequences of miscommunication that eventually lower productivity. There's a chance that projects will fail, deadlines will be missed, and job quality may suffer. This compromises not just the company's ongoing operations but also its reputation, undermining customer satisfaction and confidence.

Employee morale is also at risk from internal misunderstanding. Employee job satisfaction drops and turnover rates rise when workers feel misinformed or alienated. Excessive staff turnover hinders the development of a steady and productive work environment in addition to costing money for hiring and training new hires and interrupting business continuity.

From the outside, a lack of communication may damage ties with suppliers, customers, and other stakeholders. Inaccurate and delayed information delivery may lead to lost business, unhappy clients, and missed opportunities. Word-of-mouth spreads quickly, and unfavorable comments may damage a brand's reputation and perhaps harm its position in the market over time.

Social media magnifies the negative effects of inadequate communication in the digital era. A single error in public relations or customer service may cause a catastrophe that swiftly spreads throughout internet channels. Damage management becomes difficult, and the company could find it difficult to win back the public's faith. This might result in monetary losses and a decline in market share.

Furthermore, poor communication discourages creativity in the workplace. Ideas are stifled in a society that does not value honest and open communication. Workers could be reluctant to provide insightful opinions, which would stifle innovation and make it more difficult for the company to adjust to the needs of a changing market.

Bad communications may have a devastating effect on any firm, regardless of its size. In certain cases, the influence can be so great that it may be almost difficult to reverse the final outcomes. It is crucial to recognize that poor communication need to be minimized, if not completely eradicated. Ineffective communication may have an impact on the following areas:

Bad communication practices may have a significant impact on a company's output levels since they impede both productivity and communication. Goals and deadlines are often at jeopardy when this occurs. Ineffective communication may also result in low employee morale, which can ultimately affect the whole company platform.

Lack of awareness of expectations and underperformance will lead to a great deal of confusion and stagnation in the company's procedures, which will have a detrimental effect on the projected daily development. Errors are often made as a result of the weak or nonexistent communication abilities of individuals giving directions.

In some situations, this exacerbates the already poor communication since it starts the assigning of blame. As a result, it's critical to make sure everyone involved in a given exercise is aware of all expectations. If there are still many instances of poor communication, then some kind of readdress should be promoted in order to assist dispel any bad vibes.

In conclusion, there are many detrimental effects of inadequate communication on a company. It has an impact on internal dynamics, reduces output, lowers staff morale, strains ties with outside stakeholders, and has the potential to worsen reputation-damaging situations. It is crucial to invest in strong communication techniques and promote a transparent culture in order to protect a business's health and longevity.

CHAPTER 20:

FINAL HINT

There is communication even when you don't believe it. You need to make a gesture to indicate that you don't want to converse, because gestures are an element of communication. Cultures vary in how they communicate, and silence is one of them. In some cultures, pausing for a long time before responding to a question is considered dignified, while in others, it may be seen as foolish behavior.

This implies that body language may sometimes convey a lot more information to others than words alone when it comes to communicating. When your mother sees you coming home late, for example, you can tell by her expressions even if she doesn't say anything that she is conveying something meaningful and "grounded."

It is impossible to take back words once said, which renders all forms of communication irreversible. It is for this reason that the proverb "think before you speak" has gained popularity: once you talk, you cannot take back the benefit or cause the harm.

There is a proverb that goes, "Message will be heard in its most negative sense, if there is any," therefore you need to make sure that you're using the most positive words and phrases to avoid any unwanted consequences from your communication. This makes it quite evident that in order to communicate more effectively and positively, you should refrain from using derogatory language and idioms.

Because contextual communication involves relationships, it is possible that you will never talk in a vacuum and that you will always require someone to clarify what you are saying. It may be a buddy, a social gathering, an organizational gathering, your life partner, or anybody else, but you need someone who can interpret and respond to your messages. This adds to the intrigue since it requires you to consider the other party's point of view and adjust your communication appropriately when they are participating. You may have understood the meaning then, but you could have communicated a different meaning if you had started talking in your own manner.

One thing is clear from all of these qualities: you must communicate with extreme precision. If you omit any important details, the whole point of communicating will be lost, and you will suffer some kind of loss.

WRAPPING UP

Effective communication is really important in our daily lives, as you must have realized if you read and comprehended this eBook back then. It originates from our close personal relationships and may lead to a position as CEO of a firm. You will almost certainly need to communicate successfully at every turn in your life. Not only may poor or inadequate communication disrupt your own life, but it can also have a significant negative impact on many others.

This phenomena greatly raises the need of efficient communication. Throughout the whole eBook, you will find several methods and resources to assess your own interpersonal communication abilities, and after you have done so, you may improve them. It will take time to improve all of these talents since, as the saying goes, "Anything worthwhile, takes a while." However, improving these skills is an essential aspect of your life. Therefore, you should continue with the learning process if you have been attempting to enhance and increase the effectiveness of your communication.

Either early or late, results will materialize. You will soon be in the same position as your boss, so don't undervalue yourself by seeing some self-assured coworker who is closer to them. All you need is a little internal perfection to inspire you. It is important to emphasize that communication is a skill that can be developed through time and experience. You will become an extremely proficient communicator if you follow the above-mentioned methods to make it happen.

Ineffective communication also hinders the business's ability to grow overall as it results in a lack of advancement in terms of sales and public awareness of the company, its goods, and services. Ineffective communication may also lead to expensive misunderstandings. In an environment where poor communication is common, rejecting items because they don't live up to client criteria is not an uncommon occurrence.

Examining how you communicate in your personal, professional, and network marketing lives and asking yourself, "What is in it for each of the different personalities?" is a terrific concept. Combining it with a segmented analysis will enable you to create effective communication strategies. In our everyday lives, effective communication is incredibly important and profoundly significant. It will take time to improve all of these talents, but as they say, "Anything worthwhile, takes a while," thus it is vital that you give them more attention.